The Library of the Civil Rights Movement™

The Montgomery Bus Boycott

Integrating Public Buses

Jake Miller

The Rosen Publishing Group's
PowerKids Press™
New York

Published in 2004 by The Rosen Publishing Group, Inc.
29 East 21st Street, New York, NY 10010

First Edition
Editor: Frances E. Ruffin
Book Design: Emily Muschinske

Photo Credits: Cover and title page, 8, 15, 16, 19 © Bettmann/CORBIS, pp. 5, 11 (inset), 15 (inset) © AP/Wide World Photos; p. 6 © CORBIS; p. 11 © Grey Villet/TimePix; p. 12, 19 (inset) © Don Cravens/TimePix.

Miller, Jake, 1969–
The Montgomery bus boycott : integrating public buses / Jake Miller.—1st ed.
p. cm. — (Library of the civil rights movement)
Includes bibliographical references and index.
ISBN 0-8239-6251-2 (lib. bdg.)
1. Montgomery (Ala.)—Race relations—Juvenile literature. 2. Segregation in transportation—Alabama—Montgomery—History—20th century—Juvenile literature. 3. African Americans—Civil rights—Alabama—Montgomery—History—20th century—Juvenile literature. [1. Montgomery (Ala.)—Race relations. 2. Segregation in transportation—History. 3. African Americans—Civil rights—History.] I. Title.
F334.M79 N454 2003
323.1'196073076147—dc21

2001007239

Manufactured in the United States of America

Contents

Taking a Stand

On December 1, 1955, a quiet, polite, 42-year-old woman named Rosa Parks was arrested. Her crime was sitting in her seat on a bus. Parks was riding on one of the 62 yellow buses that rolled through the city streets of Montgomery, Alabama. She was on her way home from her job as a seamstress. When the bus got crowded, the driver ordered Rosa Parks to get out of her seat. Parks was black. In those days in Montgomery, Alabama, and in many other cities in the South, black people had to sit in the "black section" in the back of a bus. Sometimes the section in the front of the bus reserved for white people filled up. Then black riders, like Parks, who were seated in the middle of the bus, had to give up their seats so that white people could sit.

When Rosa Parks refused to give up her seat on a bus, she was arrested, fingerprinted, and fined.

Then and Now

In 1956, blacks did not have equal rights. The Montgomery bus boycott was just one way in which they fought to gain equal rights. Today blacks still hold protests, such as the Million Man March, as they continue to fight against racism.

Fighting Unfair Rules

Rosa Parks refused to give up her seat. She was tired from her long day of work, but she was also tired of being treated badly just because she was black. The year before, in 1954, the Supreme Court had ruled that it was illegal to send black and white children to separate schools. It didn't seem fair that a bus company could still **segregate** riders on its buses. When Parks refused to give up her seat, she was arrested and was taken to jail.

Parks was well known in the black community, and her arrest upset many people. Besides working as a seamstress, Parks offered her time at the local branch of the National Association for the Advancement of Colored People (**NAACP**). This organization had been fighting segregation and **racist** violence against blacks since 1909. The NAACP paid for Parks's release from jail.

This is a 1930s photograph of young members of the NAACP holding signs that invite others to join the group.

Don't Ride the Bus

At the time of Rosa Parks's arrest, a black college professor named Jo Ann Robinson had been waiting for the right moment to start a bus **boycott**. Black people in Montgomery, Alabama, had been treated badly by the bus company for many years. Robinson and a group of **activists** had decided that the black people in the city should stop riding buses until the bus company agreed to treat them fairly. Robinson thought that Parks's arrest would be a good symbol for the start of a boycott. Robinson printed posters, telling people that Rosa Parks had been arrested. Robinson urged people not to take the buses. She and members of the NAACP spread the word throughout the black community, including in barbershops and black-owned stores. Many black ministers who were organizers of the boycott asked their followers to support it, too.

Empty buses were the result of the Montgomery bus boycott.
Inset: Rosa Parks is shown walking to jail.

Getting Around Without the Bus

Keeping a bus boycott going in Montgomery was difficult. It was very hard for the black people who lived there to get to their jobs or to do errands around town. Many blacks could not afford their own cars. The people who organized the boycott started a group called the Montgomery Improvement Association (MIA). Its members tried to help people find ways to get around without using the bus. They organized **car pools**, in which many people shared a single car if they were traveling in the same direction. Other people got around by walking, hitchhiking, or riding bicycles. A few white bosses gave their workers rides to work. As difficult as it was to get around, nine out of every ten black people joined the boycott. The buses, which had been crowded, became nearly empty of passengers.

The Montgomery bus boycotters got around by walking, biking, or sharing rides. The majority of the black people in the city joined the boycott.

BAPTIST

Trying to Make a Deal

The boycotters had only a few **demands** at first. They wanted to do away with the reserved seating that forced blacks to give up their seats when a bus became crowded. They also wanted black drivers to be hired for bus routes in the black part of town. The bus company had no black drivers at all. Finally, they wanted black passengers to be treated with more courtesy. The bus company and the city's politicians did not want to make a deal. After this decision, the MIA leaders decided to fight for total **desegregation** of the buses. In court Rosa Parks had been found guilty and was sentenced to pay a fine of $10, but she **appealed** to a higher court. In February 1956, the MIA decided to take the bus company to **federal court**, to see if the national government would change Alabama's unfair laws toward black people.

Dr. Martin Luther King Jr. outlined plans for a boycott with Rosa Parks and others.

The Boycott Continues

All through the winter, the Montgomery bus boycott showed no signs of ending. The bus company was losing thousands of dollars a day from all the missing black riders. Black people were saving all of their money to support the MIA, so they couldn't afford to spend money on other things. As a result, the bus boycott hurt the business of white shopkeepers in downtown Montgomery. White politicians were getting angry that blacks were standing up to them. They told the city's police to give a lot of unfair traffic tickets to car pool drivers. They also encouraged white people to fire their black workers for supporting the boycott. Violence broke out. White racists even threw bombs at the homes and the churches of some of the leaders of the boycott.

Inset: *Martin Luther King Jr. was known for his inspiring speeches about civil rights.* Left: *Policemen and reporters visit the Bell Street Baptist Church after it was bombed by racists.*

Then and Now

In Rosa Parks's time, few government agencies protected people's civil rights. Blacks and others who believed in equal treatment for all formed their own groups. Now many public organizations defend people's rights.

Boycott Leaders Arrested

The **spokesman** for the boycotters was a young, Montgomery Baptist minister. His name was Dr. Martin Luther King Jr. He would prove to be one of the most important leaders of the **Civil Rights movement**. King was one of 90 boycotters who were arrested at the end of February 1956, for "encouraging a boycott." Montgomery's politicians were trying to crush the boycott, but the arrests backfired. Instead of being afraid and ashamed to go to jail, King and the others were proud to be fighting the unfair laws. By this time, people from outside of Montgomery were following the boycott. Reporters arrived in Montgomery. They reported the story of the boycott and of the arrests. Blacks and whites from around the world held **demonstrations** and raised money to help the blacks who were involved in the Montgomery bus boycott.

After he was found guilty for his part in the boycott, Martin Luther King Jr. was cheered as a hero. He is pictured with his wife, Coretta, on March 30, 1956, after his trial. He was fined $500.

Boycotters Win Court Case

The boycott continued through most of 1956. The people who ran the car pools continued as best they could. People struggled to find ways to get from place to place. At the same time, the MIA case against the Montgomery bus company was slowly making its way through the courts. One federal court agreed that the bus company's segregation of blacks was illegal. The bus company and the city of Montgomery appealed that decision to the Supreme Court. Finally on November 13, 1956, the Supreme Court **upheld** the lower court's decision. It declared bus segregation illegal. Although they had lost their case, Montgomery city politicians refused to desegregate the buses until they received the official paperwork from the Supreme Court. It took another month for the papers to arrive.

Rosa Parks is pictured on December 21, 1956. She was happy because this was the day that the Supreme Court ruling banning segregation took effect. Inset: *With the boycott finished, blacks once again began to ride buses.*

CAPITAL HEIGHTS
BRADLEY DRIVE
Buy! Dairy Producers
EGG NOG
2675

Desegregated Buses

On December 21, 1956, Martin Luther King Jr. and several other black leaders boarded the first desegregated bus in the history of Montgomery, Alabama. The boycott had lasted for 381 days. The black citizens of Montgomery had won their case, but their troubles were not finished. White racists were angry that the black people had won their fight. The racists reacted violently. Some racists planted bombs that exploded at the homes of boycott leaders and at black churches. **Snipers** fired guns at desegregated buses. A group of five white men beat up a young black woman who was waiting for a bus. However, even violence could not stop black people from fighting to be treated fairly. The Montgomery bus boycott was just the beginning of what would be a long fight for justice and fair treatment.

Martin Luther King Jr., seated in the second row, was one of the first blacks in Montgomery, Alabama, to ride the buses after they were desegregated.

The Movement Beyond Montgomery

After the boycott, Martin Luther King Jr. started a group called the Southern Christian Leadership Conference (SCLC). In the years that followed, King and the SCLC became powerful forces in the Civil Rights movement. With the lessons they had learned in Montgomery, people fought for more than a decade to make America a place where everyone could be treated fairly, no matter the color of his or her skin. Those early civil rights leaders and **protesters** weren't fighting alone, though. There were other civil rights causes, and many thousands of black and white people from around the country took up those causes. The people in Montgomery had walked miles (km) during a cold winter and a hot summer in pursuit of justice. People across America joined the fight for civil rights.

Glossary

activists (AK-tih-vists) People who do things like protest and demonstrate to support a cause that they believe in.

appealed (uh-PEELD) Asked a judge in a higher court to take a second look at a legal decision.

boycott (BOY-kaht) To join with others in refusing to buy from or deal with a person, a nation, or a business.

car pools (KAR POOLS) Groups of people that share a single car.

civil rights movement (SIH-vul RYTS MOOV-mint) People and groups working together to win freedom and equality for all.

demands (dih MANDZ) Requests or requirements presented by a person or a group to another person or group.

demonstrations (deh-mun-STRAY-shun) Public displays or gatherings for a person or cause.

desegregation (DEE-seh-gruh-gay-shun) The process of bringing divided groups together to end segregation.

federal court (FEH-duh-rul KORT) Court that upholds federal laws which apply to all the states in the nation, and which makes sure state courts are dealing fairly with all citizens.

NAACP National Association for the Advancement of Colored People, a group that fights for the rights of black people.

protesters (PROH-test-erz) People who take part in demonstrations.

racist (RAY-sist) A person who has the belief that one group, or race, of people, such as whites, is better than another group, such as blacks.

segregate (SEH-gruh-gayt) To separate people of different races.

snipers (SNY-purz) People who shoot guns at other people from secret hiding spots.

spokesman (SPOHKS-min) A person who talks to the public to give the views of a group.

upheld (up-HELD) Decided that the first court made the right decision.

Index

Primary Sources

Cover: Rosa Parks Riding the Bus December 21, 1956 after Supreme Court ban on segregated transportation. **Page 5:** Rosa Parks is arrested and fingerprinted (February 1956). By Gene Herrick, Associated Press. **Page 6:** Portrait of NAACP Youth Council (1930s). **Page 8:** View of an empty Montgomery bus. **Page 8 inset:** Rosa Parks walked to jail. (February 1956). **Page 11:** Blacks in Montgomery boycott buses by walking (1956). **Page 11 inset:** Church-operated cars provide transportation for boycotters. (May 1956) Associated Press. **Page 12:** Dr. Martin Luther King Jr., Ralph Abernathy and Rosa Parks plan boycott strategies. By Don Cravens (January 1956). **Page 15:** Bell Street Baptist Church, one of four black churches bombed. (January 1957). **Page 15 inset:** Dr. Martin Luther King urged a bus boycott (1956). By Gene Herrick, Associated Press. **Page 16:** Dr. Martin Luther King and his wife Coretta are cheered by a crowd. (March 1956). **Page 18:** Rosa Parks smiles after hearing of ban on segregated transportation (December 1956). **Page 18 inset:** African Americans ride the bus at the end of the bus boycott. **Page 20:** Ministers King, Abernathy, and Rev. Glenn Smiley are among the first to ride Montgomery's buses after the boycott (December 1956). Associated Press.

Web Sites

To learn more about the Montgomery bus boycott, check out these Web sites:

www.girlpower.gov/girlarea/gpguests/RosaParks.htm
www.worldbook.com/fun/aajourny/html/bh005.html